What's the Deal With...

The Talk Between Adult Children and Their Parents?

Jack Tatar

16 15 14 13   10 9 8 7 6 5 4 3 2 1

What's the Deal With...The Talk Between Adult
Children and their Parents?
ISBN-10:0991250109
ISBN-13:978-0-9912501-0-3

Library of Congress Cataloging-in-Publication Data is
available upon request.

Published by PeopleTested® Publications
www.PeopleTested.com

Contents

What Do You Need to Have a Safe Retirement?

Having a safe and lengthy retirement requires more that just being financially prepared. It also requires that retirees and pre-retirees consider the four keys to a safe retirement, which includes not only financial preparedness, but health and wellness, mental attitude and the need to stay involved as well.

Most retirement books today deal primarily with the aspects of having enough money to retire. Certainly the foundation for retirement requires a focus on being financially prepared and having a game plan providing financial security and retirement income. It's the topic that brings the most questions from those retiring or in retirement and it's the first key for a safe retirement.

The reality of considering healthcare costs in retirement is now leading more people to evaluate not only their own healthcare plan but their own health as well. To me, it's common sense that a safe and long retirement not only depends on how much money I have but also on how healthy I am. Remember that old uncle who always said, "If you don't have your health, you have nothing"? Well, he was right.

So the second key covers the vital topic of ensuring that we keep our health and wellness in check. Although everyone's situation is different and the scientific landscape keeps changing and evolving, the reality is that we now know enough about what we need to do to monitor and improve our health. If you're still smoking and not exercising in your retirement, you obviously don't care about these matters but if you'd like to fully enjoy your retirement years, the reality is that eating right and exercising are just the basics that you need to be doing.

The third key focuses on your mental attitude. As we retire, we face a new period in our lives that can be what we've worked for and dreamed about.

It can also be a time when we lose friends and family. It becomes vital for us to keep our attitude in check. No one else can tell you how to think or how to feel but do you really want to be that grumpy old man or woman who acts like they've been beaten by life and they live their retirement full of regrets, anger, and loneliness?

This is not a "safe retirement," and before long not only will this impact the enjoyment of your retirement, but it will significantly impact the length of it as well.

Retirement should be your opportunity to explore who you are and how you want to live the rest of your life. For many this may be the first time that you've been able to do this and explore, really explore, who you are and what makes you happy.

So the fourth key is all about enjoying retirement. The way to do this is to get and stay involved. Retirement is a time to celebrate, a time to live and enjoy. The way to do that is to get involved with old friends and new friends. The opportunities are limitless and range from mission trips to Asia to simply playing bingo or bridge with friends.

I believe that only through the use of all of these four keys can you unlock the safe retirement that you've worked hard to enjoy!

This section originally appeared on Marketwatch.com - http://www.marketwatch.com/story/the-four-keys-to-a-safe-retirement-2012-12-13

Have You Had "The Talk" Yet?

No, this is not the one in which the parents talk to their kids about sex and hope that they actually still know more than their kids on the topic.

This "talk" also includes parents and children but the concerns are different and are related to retirement and aging: medical proxies, healthcare and estate planning, wills, trusts, and the fact that 70% of people over age 65 will require some form of long-term care.

Given the inevitability of our aging process and the concerns that people have about thriving and living safely in retirement, a recent American Association of Retired Persons (AARP) survey found that two-thirds of adult children have never talked about these matters with their parents.

A recent Fidelity study, "*shows adult children and their parents struggle to communicate on key financial topics that include retirement planning, providing care for elderly parents and inheritance strategies. The study analyzed levels of disagreement and miscommunication between parents and their adult children on a range of sensitive topics, and found that adult children are not only anxious about their own finances, but also their parents' future health, retirement security and estate plan.*"[1]

As the child of retiring parents, it should be rewarding to watch your parents enter this new phase of their lives. It's a time to celebrate their labors and efforts. It's a time in which you can help your parents achieve what they've always dreamed of doing in much the same way they helped you to achieve your dreams. In order to achieve this, you will need to be an active participant in the discussion, planning and implementation phase of your parents' retirement and their later years.

More than likely you will eventually have the talk with your parents; but often it happens too late, when you're operating in crisis mode and often with a parent with diminished mental capacities. You can also run into situations where more than one sibling is involved, or even children from different marriages and unspoken expectations can exist. These are much better flushed out and dealt with head on. The goal should be: the earlier the better!

The best time to have the talk is well before you need it. Ideally, even before your parents have retired. This will allow for a richer and more intelligent conversation. Retiring successfully entails far more than just having a set number of dollars in your savings account.

Those people happiest in their retirement years have not only financial health, but they stay physically fit and eat right, look after their mental acumen and attitude, and have close relationships with friends and family. These are all topics that you should cover in the talk.

---

1 http://www.fidelity.com/inside-fidelity/individual-investing/intra-family-generational-finance-study

The reality is that crises can happen at any age. So it's important to recognize that although this is a conversation that will be tough to have, it needs to be done. The reality is also that your parents may be waiting for you to begin the discussion. Having the talk will provide peace of mind to both you and them!

And if you're a retiree reading this who feels invincible and doesn't have the impending need to discuss these matters, remember that life can be fragile. I'm sure you can think of a friend or family member who has proven this to you.

To you I say, if your children haven't initiated the talk, reach out to them. You've always been a leader to them and this may need to be another matter that you have to take the lead on.

This section originally appeared on Marketwatch.com - http://www.marketwatch.com/story/having-the-talk-about-retirement-2012-12-24

How Do I Have the Talk?

Well, the first thing we *don't* want to do is start with something like, "Hey mom, we need to discuss when you'll move into a nursing home, who you're leaving your money and the house to, and what kind of memorial service you want?"

Yikes!

Put yourself in your parents' shoes. Most people of their generation were raised never speaking about money or other personal issues except with their spouses. Somewhere along the way it became taboo in our culture, and this only serves to make things more difficult.

Remember, having the talk does not mean controlling anyone's life or giving up control of your own. It also doesn't mean being critical of any situation your parents have found themselves in. If they haven't set themselves up perfectly for retirement and they need some help, don't be judgmental. Just remind yourself of how many times you've messed things up and hoped no one noticed.

The key word here is *respect*. Congratulate your parents on achieving everything they've done (including creating and raising a brilliant child like yourself). You're here to help in any way you can. In order to help, you first need to understand. This can be a good way to introduce the need for the talk.

Below I've outlined key areas to consider and apply for how to have the talk. Just as going for a swim in a cool ocean, the first plunge is always the hardest. After that, each stroke gets easier, and before you know it, you don't even notice the cold.

Goals

For adult children, before you even begin the talk, make sure your goals are in line with your parents'. It's their money, not yours (even though it may be one day). You're discussing their lives, not yours. This may sound obvious, but it's easy to lose sight of what we're really talking about. A simple reminder of this will help shift the focus directly onto your parents or loved ones, rather than onto yourself.

A good approach is, "I want to make sure I can help you with whatever you need help with."

The end goal is to create a beginning. You're laying the groundwork for further communication, and the information and decisions will happen bit by bit over time. These discussions make it much, much easier.

By having these discussions, you're actually helping to remove a burden from your parents. The reality is that a goal of theirs is to ensure they're able to take care of their family as they get older.

Time the Talk

The talk needs to be timed in two ways. Adult children should consider what the relative age and well being of their parents is. If they're still working and vital, maybe you can put it off a few years until they're more ready themselves to think of retirement. This is a fine line because you don't want to put it off until a crisis of some sort has already happened.

However, if you're ready to get started, you must also consider the specific timing. The right time is probably not at Thanksgiving dinner with a table full of people. Nor is it at the county fair barbecue, when they're surrounded by friends and acquaintances.

Pick a quiet and comfortable location, and make sure you all have enough time that no one has to jump up and leave. Consider having coffee or lunch together to set the stage.

Address your concerns and tell them you want to help. Clearly explain that no one wants to take control from them. In fact, consider saying, "I need you to stay in charge." It's true. It's their life and their decisions. You're here to help.

You may find that your parents are eager to have this discussion with you and will welcome your initiative to make it happen.

Involve Other Family Members

Do this early and before you have the talk, so that everyone's concerns can be addressed. It may be effective to designate one person to have the discussions, or you may want to have all siblings there. But remember, you don't want this to feel like an intervention, and you don't want your parents or loved ones to feel like they're being ganged up on.

Whether you go it alone or with your siblings, your parents will need to be assured that all of their children are aware that this discussion is happening and that everyone is "in sync" with it. The worst thing you can do is to have this discussion without your other family members aware of it. It will cause ill will and put your parents in a bad position.

Don't do it alone. The talk is a family matter and must be treated as such.

It's Only a Beginning

Remember, this will be the first of many conversations. You don't have to get everything discussed and agreed upon in one short hour. There's no need to convince anyone of anything. You simply want to get the conversation started so you can revisit it over time.

In fact, the only thing you may accomplish in the first talk is to begin the process. It may require that you leave some information or resources with your parents and ask if you can pick up the discussion at another time after they've had more time to think about what you've said. This is okay!

I've heard from many people that they began the discussion with their parents and after leaving some materials, their parents called them a few weeks later and asked to speak with them further. At that next meeting the parents brought account statements, filled out questionnaires, and many wonderful thoughts about how they would like their retirement years to be.

The talk is never a one shot deal. It will take many discussions and should be ongoing. The important part is to take the first step and begin it.

Use an Icebreaker

For some, using an icebreaker is a great way to get the ball rolling. Here are some ideas for segueing into the talk:

- Explain that you and your spouse/significant other have just created a will or done some estate planning, and you'd like to tell them about it. Maybe you have questions and need their advice. If you're open about what you're doing, this might make them feel more comfortable about opening up, too.

- If the above doesn't apply, talk about a friend who's in a similar situation. Maybe they're worried about a parent. "My friend Mary's mother isn't recovering well from her surgery and it turns out they haven't done any estate planning at all. Have you and dad talked about this?"

- Discuss something you heard in the news or read in an article or book that raised your concerns about this topic.

Be direct. Explain that these have brought up concerns of yours and that you want to talk about them. Again, clarify that you don't want to make any decisions for them, but you do want to understand what they've done about these issues and how you can help. As well, over time you will be able to bring up ideas and issues that they most probably haven't thought of.

Listen

As simple as this sounds, it's often one of our least used communication skills. We live in a get-it-done-fast society, but our parents are entering a stage when their world is slowing down and going inward. Don't pressure your parents to hurry up. Instead, allow for lots of time. And most importantly, listen to what they have to say and want to do.

This will be the time that you'll need the skill of active listening, which basically means that you'll need to be fully engaged in the discussion with your parents. This should include a confirmation of what they've said by recapping it in your own words. This will confirm that you've heard what they're saying and that they've been heard. This is critical to ensure that there have been no misunderstandings or misconceptions.

It's also important that you show "active concern" for both of your parents during the discussion. Don't assume that their finances are something that only your dad has a handle on. You need to ensure that both your dad and mom are actively included in this discussion and that their points of view and opinions have been expressed.

If you don't feel both parents have been effectively heard from, this may require an additional conversation with each parent, and you may find yourself playing an intermediary role. The best approach is to ensure that you hear from each parent when they are together and everyone agrees with what has been said. The skill of active listening will help here.

Be Respectful

Your parents have worked hard to be at the point in their lives where they can successfully consider retiring. This is something to celebrate and be proud of. In the same way that they have been proud of you for your accomplishments throughout your life, you should now be proud of what they have accomplished.

So you need to be respectful of their decisions, opinions, and thoughts throughout this process. Always.

At the end of the day you have no legal right to make any decisions for them. Nor do you have an obligation. What you can do, though, is understand where they are in their financial, health, attitude, and social worlds. If they're not where they want to be or should be, you can help them get there.

Reassure them that you're not going to take away control, but you do have concerns. When talking to your parents, it's good to take note of how David Solie defines control: "*A primary human desire at all stages of life that becomes an all consuming driver of behavior in senior adults as they cope with profound losses on a daily basis.*"[2]

Using this definition, you can see the benefits once again of having the talk at an earlier time in your parents' retirement life. As Solie further points out, the loss of control shows itself as, "*the waning of strength, health, peer group members and consultative authority as a person ages, compelling that person to fight to retain whatever does remain under the person's control.*"[3]

Back Off

The response you get from the first talk will vary. Some parents will resist and feel uncomfortable. "It's all taken care of, don't you worry." Others will share their concerns easily,

2 David Solie, *How to Say It to Seniors: Closing the Communication Gap with Our Elders*, (Upper Saddle River, NJ: Prentice Hall Press, 2004) - Please visit his Web site for more information and valuable resources at http://www.DavidSolie. com .
3 *Ibid.*

and the rest will land somewhere in between. Either way, you've opened the door for more conversations.

If they are resistant, back off. Pressuring someone into something is almost never the right move. If you badger them you'll most likely alienate them rather than bring them closer.

Let it rest. See how things go. This will be a process.

You can always revisit the talk again at a later date. This is especially true if a triggering event occurs, like reoccurring missed bills, an accident at home, or the onset of an illness.

Having the talk isn't that difficult, it just seems that way at the beginning. If you keep at the foremost of your mind that you're there to help, not to take anything away from them, this will permeate the conversation.

It's my profound belief that both you and your parents will be greatly satisfied with the results of having the talk. These will include a closer relationship between you and your parents, greater certainty that you'll make decisions for your aging parents that are based upon what they truly want, and you'll improve their ability to live a safe retirement.

*This section is from "**Having the Talk: The Four Keys to Your Parents' Safe Retirement**"* [4]

---

4 http://talk.peopletested.com

What are the Six Vital Questions to Ask?

Each year as the holidays are coming to an end and a new year beckons, resolutions will be made and broken. You really don't have to wait until the beginning of the year to think about what does the future hold for you? What does it hold for your family?

If you're a retiree or someone planning on retirement, the questions and concerns that you have about the future will be many. Most will focus on issues of finances, healthcare and health. For the family members of those retirees or soon to be retirees, their concerns will more than likely become your concerns as well.

Those in the sandwich generation are not only dealing with their own needs and the needs of their children, but the needs of their parents as well. Questions and concerns about end of life care, social security, medical decisions, wills, trusts, and estate planning are hitting many adult children sooner than they planned because they have to play a role with their own parents to address these questions.

If you're in this situation, it's important to begin the talk about these matters with your retired or retiring parents as part of your plans for the future. Although the foundation of this talk will be around the financial matters, it should not be limited to these points only.

A necessary beginning step of the talk is to work with your parents to gather all current financial information and identify all of the points of contact for their accounts such as any names of advisors, accountants, etc. Any work already done regarding estate planning considerations such as trusts, wills, etc. should also be included.

In order to ensure that you get off on the right foot with these discussions, here are some of the questions that you should be asking of your parents at this early stage of the talk:

1) Do you have a will? If so, when was it last updated?

2) Have you established a trust or done other more extensive financial planning?

3) Do you have a current list of assets, passwords, and important documents and where they are held?

4) Do you have a thorough financial plan in place outlining your financial needs, goals, and strategies throughout retirement? And, most importantly, when was the last time that your reviewed it?

5) When is the last time you updated the beneficiaries on your retirement accounts, annuities, life insurance, etc?

If your parents have a trusted advisor that they work with, you may want to involve them in these discussions as well. They can often be a vital intermediary during these discussions or they can be a valuable resource after you've gone through this information with your parents.

I often advise advisors to ask the following question of their retiring or retired clients who they sense have not had the necessary intergenerational talk:

"Have you discussed your wishes with the executor of your estate?"

The answer to this can either lead to a joint discussion involving that executor and their parents or it can lead to the necessary discussion that needs to take place with that executor.

Either way, it's a question that can lead to having the talk and if you're an advisor, I recommend asking it of your clients who are retired or retiring.

If you're a retiree or soon to be retiree, ask yourself that question and get the ball rolling on initiating the talk. It's not important who begins it, just that it happens.

If you're an adult child of a retiring or retired parent, I hope that you'll put the talk not only on your list of New Year's resolution, but on your "to-do" list for tomorrow.

The best thing you can do is to just do it and get the ball rolling now. It's not just for your benefit but for those you love as well.

This section originally appeared on Marketwatch.com - http://www.marketwatch.com/story/questions-you-should-ask-your-parents-2012-12-31

What are the Danger Signs for Elderly Investors?

Adult children of retirees and pre-retirees need to speak with their parents earlier, rather than later, about retirement and the need to address financial and life matters.

That's the major take-away of my book, "**Having The Talk: The Four Keys to Your Parents' Safe Retirement**."[5] It's a difficult discussion to have and that's why most of us put it off until it's too late.

Ultimately most of us end up having the conversation with our parents at some point but it's often at a time when their mental capacities are diminished or there are expectations that have been unspoken that can cause life long rifts in families.

It's a big part of my overall message to my multigenerational audiences: have the talk with your parents about retirement earlier than you think you should. By doing so, you set up plans and structures to address the issues that will arise in later years and the reality is that parents are more willing to do this and live in comfort knowing that this will be one less issue they'll have to deal with as they grow older.

---

5 http://talk.peopletested.com

Now the facts are bearing out the need for having these discussions earlier. Michael Finke of Texas Tech University published a sudy in 2011 that shows *"that older respondents experience a decline in cognitive processes closely related to financial decision making. Financial literacy scores decline by about 2% each year after age 60. Confidence in financial decision making abilities does not decline with age. Increasing confidence and reduced abilities can explain poor credit and investment choices by older respondents."*[6]

Finke's study shows that although the financial literacy of those over 60 decreases, their level of confidence doesn't, which can make for some poor investment and credit decisions at a time when these choices can cause havoc in a retiree's portfolio. These choices and decisions result in closed accounts, damaged credit, money lost to scam artists, foreclosure and ultimately can ruin any financial plan that a retiree has put together to allow them to live out their golden years.

As we age, many of us simply refer to strange behavior or forgetfulness as "senior moments". As I write in my book, *"Old age can be overwhelming. It's not just the physical changes— the creaky knees and aches and pains that predict rain better than any meteorologist—but also the mind slows down. We've all experienced it even if we're still in our roaring 40s. We even refer to them as "senior moments."*

To a certain extent this is actually a healthy aspect of aging, because it allows the person to begin the reflection process that helps them figure out the meaning of their life. But when the slowing mind gets in the way of managing the

6 http://papers.ssrn.com/sol3/papers.cfm?abstract_id=1948627

financial, health, or safety aspects of living, this previously benevolent characteristic turns into a danger."[7]

Invariably, strange or irregular behavior in our later years can lead many to wonder, "is it Alzheimer's?" (I remind you that Alzheimer's is a disease and not something that occurs because you age) When you add in the challenges and concerns about Alzheimer's into the equation for our aging parents, it further reinforces the need for earlier discussion about retirement. In an article by Glen Ruffenach, the point is made that this problem is magnified by the harsh facts: "*The numbers are scary: One in eight Americans age 65 and over and 43 percent of individuals 85 and over have Alzheimer's disease. Every 69 seconds, on average, someone in the U.S. develops the illness. But financial advisers and accountants, when asked about their experiences with clients who have memory loss, invariably raise the same concern: Elderly parents and adult children alike are too slow to seek or provide help in the early stages of decline.*"[8]

So how can we identify these "early stages of decline"? In his article, Ruffenbach, points out some of the danger signs to look for:

- Be on the lookout for seniors giving out credit card information on the phone—this can often be the sign that they are being targeted for financial scams on the elderly who often see calls as a way to stay connected to the outside world.

---

7 http://talk.peopletested.com

8 http://www.marketwatch.com/story/talking-to-mom-about-alzheimers-and-her-money-1335192298522

- A large number of phone solicitations and donation requests in the mailbox may also be another danger sign.

- Any discussions about making major changes to their portfolio without the existence of a plan is also another danger sign.

In my book, I point out that family members should be on the lookout for these "red flags" with their parents and loved ones that something is not right and that a situation with that family member needs to be addressed:

- Worsening health issues that are painful and/or effect mobility

- Trouble with previously routine tasks such as balancing a checkbook

- An increase in forgetfulness such as missing bill payments

- Cognitive impairment that goes beyond normal "senior moments"

- A decrease in personal hygiene

- Trouble keeping the home clean and repaired

- A tendency toward depression and isolation[9]

These red flags can indicate a more serious situation than just "senior moments" and should be addressed immediately and appropriately. The damage to ones health is the first thing to be addressed, but you also need to recognize the impact that this can cause for that person's, and their family's financial situation as well if this is addressed too late.

---

9 https://talk.peopletested.com

Once again, I have to bring it back to the need to have the talk and discussions about finances and later life decisions earlier rather than later. Having these discussions at a time of crisis is unfortunately when most of us do have these discussions, but any one who has been through that will tell you the same thing—"I wish that I had discussed these matters early with my parents!"

Ensure that all proper documentation has been secured and set up a helpful and necessary program to review your loved ones' finances that focuses on how you're protecting them.

Another case for discussing the topic of financial assistance with parents early is clarified by Kiki Brink (a former college professor who worked with dementia patients in hospice settings before starting her own personal-administrator service in Salem, Ore.) , "*If you suddenly step in and take control, without any prior give and take, parents feel belittled," she says. But "if you get in early, you haven't taken away their dignity.*"[10]

Is this an easy thing to do? No. Is it necessary? I hope that you see that it is!

Those familiar with my writings and appearances[11] know that there can be many conversation starters and methods to get the talk started. They include sharing stories about friends, neighbors or others that they can relate to about what could happen to them in their advanced age and above all, stressing that having these discussions is all about helping them now as they have always helped you.

10 http://www.marketwatch.com/story/talking-to-mom-about-alzheimers-and-her-money-1335192298522

11 http://www.safe4retirement.com

But however you do it, the point is to "just do it!" The reality is that the role that you can play for your parents and loved ones as they age is an important and necessary aspect of your life, much as their role helping you to grow up was to them.

This section originally appeared on Marketwatch.com - http://www.marketwatch.com/story/the-talk-danger-signs-for-elderly-investors-2013-03-11

How Can You Protect Seniors from Identity Theft?

My dad was a stickler about identity fraud.

He would have special pens that would thwart check fraudsters. He would lecture me about my use (or misuse) of envelopes that weren't "security" envelopes. Like any son, I would think that he was a bit over the top about his concerns and didn't pay attention to yet another of the valuable lessons that he tried to convey to me.

However, with more and more stories about retirees having identity fraud experiences, it's important to take notice. The Internet Crime Complaint Center claims that 35% of identity theft complaints come from those aged 50 or older.[12] A survey by Experian found that "*11% of people over the age of 65 reported that they have had their financial information stolen.*" [13]

The belief is that many retirees and seniors are targets because they have higher cash reserves and are often less

12 http://www.ic3.gov/media/annualreport/2011_ic3report.pdf
13 http://www.silverplanet.com/scams/identity-theft/seniors-are-easy-targets-id-thieves/55337#.Unp1lBZJDlo

technologically savvy than others. But this is not just an online issue.

The stories about "long lost" relatives calling seniors for money over the phone is a regular activity of con artists today. Believe me, when your nephew or grandchild calls and you are unsure of the sound of their voice (or the reason for their call), it's as likely to be legitimate as that $500,000 that the Kingdom of Nairobi is going to send you just because they like you.

The story gets even sadder when you learn that a growing place for identity theft is in retirement homes where staff members with access to resident records are selling social security numbers and other personal information to thieves.

So how do you protect yourself?

The following steps can help make protect retirees and seniors from identity theft:

- Buy a shredder and use it for anything that has personal data on it.

- Don't keep your social security card, pin numbers, or passwords in your wallet or billfold.

- If you're doing online banking, make sure you only use reputable and secure sites. Two clues are an "s" after the "http" in the website address, and the little yellow lock that appears in the lower tool bar.

- Avoid "phishing" emails that appear to come from the bank or financial institution but are just devious ways to get you to give out their personal information.

- Mail any letters with personal details, such as their social security number or account details, from post office collection boxes rather than unguarded personal mailboxes (which can provide a convenient place for the bad guys to steal your information).

- Keep copies of your credit cards, social security cards, and other important documents in a safe but accessible (only to you and a loved one) place at home. If a credit card is stolen, you'll have the correct phone numbers at hand to cancel the cards.

- Monitor your bank statements regularly. This way if any suspicious charges come up you can act immediately.

- Cellphones, iPads, and other cool technology are also great targets for thieves. We live in a world now where someone can walk by your outdoor Starbucks table and swipe your cellphone without you even noticing.

- One of the more sad precautions to take is to limit information when writing obituaries for relatives. Con artists will often troll the obit section of local papers in order to create their new (illegal) persona.

I just ordered a new box of envelopes for myself. Yes, they were security envelopes.

Here are some articles of value to provide further information on this topic:

- Twelve steps to take when you encounter identity theft[14]

---

14 http://www.bankrate.com/finance/financial-literacy/12-steps-for-victims-of-identity-fraud-1.aspx

- How a neighbor stole your identity[15]

- Hacker-proof your password[16]

- Beware scams preying on your charitable instincts[17]

This section originally appeared on Marketwatch.com -
http://www.marketwatch.com/story/9-ways-to-protect-seniors-
from-identity-theft-2013-01-03

---

15 http://www.marketwatch.com/story/how-a-neighbor-stole-your-identity-
2012-12-10

16 http://www.marketwatch.com/story/beware-scams-preying-on-your-
charitable-instincts-2012-12-21

17 http://www.marketwatch.com/story/beware-scams-preying-on-your-
charitable-instincts-2012-12-21

What are the 5 Critical Health Questions to Ask?

Having the talk with your parents about retirement and aging usually finds people primarily focusing on the financial aspects such as wills, estates, and financial considerations for care in one's later years.

If you've gotten through that part of the talk, congratulations!

However, the talk has a number of parts to it and what is often the toughest to talk about, but may be the most important one to have, is the focus on the health needs for retirees and seniors.

According to a recent AARP study, only 26% of 65-74-year-olds partake in regular physical activity. After the age of 70 it gets worse; only 16% are active regularly.[18] This can be bad news indeed for long-term health and is something that needs to be discussed during the talk.

After all, common sense tells us that if you don't feel good in retirement, you won't enjoy it as much and matters related to health, including exercise, need to be discussed and incorporated into any retirement plan.

---

18 http://assets.aarp.org/rgcenter/general/exercise-bulletin-survey.pdf

It's no secret that discussing health with your parents can be a difficult thing. I know that it was for me. However, there are many times I wish I'd discussed with my parents their need to exercise and to involve me in their health decisions. I didn't have these discussions and my mom passed away with an illness that she shielded her entire family from. Having these discussions can prevent this from happening to you.

These discussions may not be easy to start, but there can be openings or ice breakers to help bring up these topics. Often a recent health issue for a parent or friend or family member can provide the opportunity. Parents will often look to their educated, and hopefully healthy, child as a resource in discussing the latest in the area of health and eating well.

Here are five questions that should be discussed with your retiring or retired parents during the "health" part of the talk:

1) **Do you have regular physical checkups?**

   Who are the doctors that you work with? Create a list and put reminders of your parents' checkups on your own calendar.

2) **Do you have an updated list of all the medications you take?**

   Spend some time ensuring that your parents aren't using out dated or expired medications. Make sure that you become aware of all existing medical conditions and any prescribed treatments for your parents.

3) **Have you made absolutely clear to your family members your end-of life wishes?**

This includes when and if they should terminate life support, and do you have an Advanced Health Care Directive?

4) **Do you have stress in your life, and if so, do you have a plan for eliminating as much of it as possible?**

5) **How healthy is your diet and what are your plans for getting some regular exercise?**

Remember that for all of us, regardless of age, body and mind are inextricably intertwined. When your parents feel good mentally and are happy, they have more energy and want to do more things. When they feel great physically, their mind is clearer and their thoughts are more positive. This will lead to a safe and long retirement.

For retirees, remember that a healthy retirement also means a happy one. Be open to discussing these matters with your loved ones, they can be part of the process and will be very willing to help out in whatever way possible. This doesn't mean being a burden, it means letting people who care about you know what's going on. This way you also have the opportunity to share all of the good things you're discovering in your retired life with others for as long a time as possible.

This section originally appeared on Marketwatch.com - http://www.marketwatch.com/story/5-critical-health-questions-to-ask-parents-2013-01-10

Should We Discuss Long Term Care Planning?

In business, partners must protect themselves from the financial ramifications that a significant health or lifestyle change of a partner can have on the other.

To protect themselves, business owners form a "buy/sell agreement" as a kind of "insurance" against these events, which cannot only place a significant burden on one partner, but can cripple a company as well.

According to Wikipedia, a buy/sell agreement "*is a legally binding agreement between co-owners of a business that governs the situation if a co-owner dies or is otherwise forced to leave the business, or chooses to leave the business.*"[19]

I like to think of this type of agreement as a business continuation agreement. When one partner has either died or is unable to remain in the business, the value of the business and the financial wellbeing of the other partner is ensured.

Robert Wood, a contributor to Forbes magazine, writes that this kind of "*agreement can ward off infighting by family members, co-owners and spouses, keep the business afloat*

19 http://en.wikipedia.org/wiki/Buy–sell_agreement

so its goodwill and customer base remain intact, and avoid liquidity problems."[20]

Mike Padawer, who is a leading adviser in the area of long-term care planning, believes that "*if you take a simplistic view of the relationship of couples, it's actually very similar to the relationship between partners in a business. In a business relationship, there are financial ramifications on one partner in the event of death, incapacitation, divorce, bankruptcy or retirement; and this is precisely why smart business partners implement a "buy/sell agreement.*""[21]

Recently, Fidelity Investments release their annual report on health care expenses in retirement, and concluded that the average couple (age 65) will need to spend approximately $240,000 on out-of-pocket healthcare expenses during their retirement years.[22] However, that figures does NOT include potential long-term care (LTC) expenses in their calculations. Given the fact that nearly 70% of all retirees will require some form of LTC services during retirement, the need for Long-Term Care planning becomes evident when you consider its impact upon a family and their wealth.

Mr. Padawer points out that "*when discussing potential LTC needs, it's very important to understand how and where care can and will be provided. LTC services range from basic care in the home to full-scale medical care in a nursing home. The majority of LTC services provide assistance with "Activities of Daily Living" (ADL), such as dressing, bathing,*

20 http://www.forbes.com/sites/robertwood/2011/02/07/in-business-get-a-buy-sell-agreement/

21 http://www.inertia-asg.com/about-inertia/

22 http://www.fidelity.com/inside-fidelity/individual-investing/retiree-health-care-costs-2012

eating, transferring, and toileting. Those who have difficulty performing two or more of the ADLs, due to physical limitations, severe cognitive impairment, or both, are generally considered to be in need of LTC services."

He advises his clients that planning for long term care will protect the well being, both financially and physically, of both partners, and he also sees this type of planning as protecting the ongoing "continuation" of the family's finances, in much the same way that a buy/sell agreement functions as a business continuation agreement for business partners.

Regardless of whether you view it as a "couple's buy/sell agreement," or simply long-term care planning, it should be done as early as possible and become a component of one's financial and retirement planning.

The mistake that we often make with long-term care planning is that we put it off as it's an expense we don't want to deal with. However, in much the same way as the hard work and dreams that owners put in their business can be derailed by not planning for physical calamities that can occur, the finances and dreams of a family can be impacted by not planning for similar physical calamities.

Mr. Padawer's message is clear, *"Don't make the mistake and put off planning until it's too late. As you, your loved ones or your clients prepare for the future, proper planning today for an uncertain tomorrow can help ensure a secure retirement and long-term financial goals."*

To help you to prepare for the consideration of long-term care for your own and your family's plans for later life, I want to highlight some resources that may help you:

- Genworth Financial, which is a leader in the long-term care product area, has information that helps you with specific LTC information based on your state.[23]

- A Kiplinger's Personal Finance reprint on the most asked questions about Long-Term Care.[24]

- The American Association for Long-Term Care Insurance provides 5 guides for consumers about long-term care.[25],

- There's even a government website that's up on the topic—this one seems to be more stable and accessible than other health-care sites that the government has put into place.[26]

I mentioned Mike Padawer[27] and his book, which is called **"What's the Deal with Long-Term Care?"**[28] is a good primer on the subject.

Full disclosure: I wrote the preface for Mike's book and as I'm by no means an expert on the subject, I simply related my own experience in the book when looking for long-term care insurance: "*I can speak from my own experience that the decision and discussions about long-term care planning are often complex and stressful. They involve thinking about the*

23 https://www.genworth.com/long-term-care-insurance/source/make-a-plan.html?iid=gnw:Home:tab:LTC:Makeaplan

24 http://www.aaltci.org/long-term-care-insurance-costs/

25 http://www.aaltci.org/long-term-care-insurance-costs/

26 http://longtermcare.gov

27 http://www.WhatstheDealwithLTC.com

28 http://www.amazon.com/Whats-Deal-Long-Term-Care-Padawer/dp/0985082070/ref=sr_1_1?ie=UTF8&qid=1383066110&sr=8-1&keywords=what%27s+the+deal+with+long+term+care

possibility that you or a loved one may become incapacitated and require extensive care in your later years. When I considered long-term care for my wife and me, we were stunned at the costs and complexity involved. At the end of the process, I was amazed at the feeling that we came away with after my wife and I had made our decision on long-term care solutions; it was the feeling of peace of mind that we had."

Learning about and evaluating long-term care options can be a difficult process. Preparing for the talk can be a great time to begin this process. At the end of it, I hope that you'll achieve the same peace of mind that I had, whatever you decide.

This section originally appeared on Marketwatch.com - http://www.marketwatch.com/story/long-term-care-planning-too-often-ignored-2013-06-26

How Can You Find Purpose in Retirement?

A recent study by Fidelity found that "*sixty-five percent of adult children and parents agree that discussing retirement readiness is an important topic, but 72 percent disagree on the level of detail that has been covered to date; and only 11 percent of children believe the conversations were very detailed.*"[29]

One thing I've learned in my work with retirement and seeing people live longer and safer in retirement is that attitude is a key driver for success. A positive attitude and having purpose in retirement are "details" that can create a safe retirement and they need to be including as part of "the talk" between adult children and their retiring or retired parents.

A recent study by the Rush University Medical Center's Alzheimer's Disease Center reveals that having purpose in ones life in later years showed a "*30% slower rate of cognitive decline than those who did not.*" Dr. Patricia Boyle of the Center in an article by Diane Cole, goes on to say that, "*having*

---

29 http://www.fidelity.com/inside-fidelity/individual-investing/intra-family-genera-tional-finance-study

purpose reduced the risk of Alzheimer's and its precursor, mild cognitive impairment."[30]

As those who are familiar with my writings know that I'm a firm believer in approaching retirement from a holistic perspective, not just from a financial focus. The conversations between adult children and retiring or retired parents related to retirement should also be holistically based.

Dr. Boyle makes the point very well when she points out that for retirees, *"..if you're pursuing goals, you're probably engaging in a whole host of behaviors that we know to be beneficial for health, such as being socially involved and connected to other people and going out and being physically active."*

The need to discuss and examine one's attitude and their outlook on life are important aspects of the transition to retirement.

The third portion of the talk should consider the mental attitude of the retiring or retired parent. I often find that a good way to begin this topic is to ask your parents if they know of anyone whose retirement they would like to emulate. It may be a celebrity, family member, or friend, but this can often lead to a nice discussion about how they would like their retirement to be and how they would like to feel in retirement.

During the mental attitude part of the talk you should discuss the following:

1. If you're not yet retired, what have you done to prepare yourself for the seismic shift in lifestyle you're about to experience?

30 http://online.wsj.com/news/articles/SB1000142412788732331680457816350
1792318298

2. If you're retired, are you generally happy and looking forward to each day?

3. In general, do you reminisce over positive or negative memories?

4. Do you give yourself mentally stimulating tasks, like business consulting, crossword puzzles, learning a new language, or taking courses?

5. Do you associate mainly with positive or negative people?

6. What do you want to do with the rest of your life?

7. Do you have a purpose in mind for what you'll do in retirement?

Retiring and getting older will come with its challenges but maintaining a positive attitude and approach to life will have as much to do with living a longer and safer retirement as having a balanced financial portfolio. It's important to consider them both as integral parts of any one's retirement plan.

Remember the answers lie in the details. Don't leave them out when you have the talk.

This section originally appeared on Marketwatch.com - http://www.marketwatch.com/story/the-talk-having-purpose-in-retirement-2013-01-30

How Do You Leave a Legacy in Retirement?

In the process of writing my book, "**Having The Talk: The Four Keys to Your Parent's Safe Retirement**",[31] I've found that one of the ways that adult children can connect with their retiring or retired parents is to view the process of creating a legacy for them as a very fulfilling project that can be jointly undertaken.

The reality is that as we retire and get older there's a need to understand the legacy that we'll leave behind.

As my good friend and expert of communication with the elderly, David Solie puts it in his book, "**How to Say it to Seniors: Closing the Communication Gap with Our Elders**," "*Every day, whether they are millionaire moguls or retired postal clerks, former CEOs or homemakers par excellence, our elders are engaged in an elaborate process of reviewing their lives to find something of meaning that will last long after they depart.*"[32]

Leaving a legacy goes beyond just the financial and philanthropic gifts we leave behind. A legacy can just be the

31 http://talk.peopletested.com
32 http://www.davidsolie.com/what-is-in-the-book.html

stories and memories that you leave with our friends and families that forever remind them of who you are.

Documenting this legacy can be a worthwhile and compelling experience for families to do together.

For the adult child, an easy way to start is to ask your parents questions about their life and let them work out the levels of importance. We tend to think of our parents as only filling that role of parenting, but actually, they've worn just as many hats as you have-maybe more. Encourage them to talk about their lives; what they've achieved and how they did it.

There's a wealth of resources that are available to people and families interested in compiling "legacies." One of the leaders in the area of helping others to create legacies is the Legacy Project.[33] They have a resource called "Across Generations"[34] which includes questionnaires that can be used when interviewing our older family members. These questionnaires include questions such as:

- Can you describe the neighborhood that you grew up in?

- What was the best gift you received growing up?

- What did you want to be growing up?

- Who has been the most significant person in your life?

- What was the happiest time in your life?

- What has been your greatest accomplishment?

- Share with us a story that you've never told us.

33 http://www.legacyproject.org

34 http://www.legacyproject.org/programs/acrossgen.html

I've also heard from adult children who have gone through this process that another way to handle this process is also to allow their parents to ask questions of each other. Among some of the questions that I've heard couples asking of each of other are the following:

- What would you do in retirement if you were not worried what anyone else might think about it?

- Is there anyone whose retirement you admire and hope that your retirement will be like theirs? Who and what about their retirement do you wish to emulate?

- What's your "bucket list"?

Remember that these are not only questions that will help your parents to understand more about what they want in their retirement, but it'll allow them to know each other even better.

Imagine that. Providing an opportunity for your parents to learn new things about each other after all of these years can be a priceless experience.

There are many other resources that can help in recording legacies for your family. Lettice Stuart was an accomplished writer and reporter with the New York Times who had all of skills to record the legacies of her family: "*their stories, their thoughts and feelings about death, life and family.*"[35] Unfortunately she lost both of her parents in the course of two years and she never had the opportunity to do that. So in 1996, she started her business, Portraits in Words to help people record what she did not. Portraits in Words produces both printed books and videos that capture family memories.

---

35 http://www.portraitsinwords.com

You can also find someone at the website for the Association of Personal Historians[36] (now doesn't that sound like a group of people who are not only good listeners but have heard many great stories? Not a bad way to earn a living, I think!). Their vision "quite simply, is a world in which the story of every person, family, community, and organization is recorded and preserved. " Not a bad vision to aspire to!

To all the adult children of retired and retiring parents, however you go about helping your parents to tell the story of their lives, remember that it's fundamental to easing them into a successful retirement and it'll provide joy for both you and them.

I promise you'll hear amazing stories that will open new windows into who your parents really are.

I think of the time when I asked my dad in his later years about his experience in the Navy. He was on an aircraft carrier called the USS Guadalcanal. His job was to work on the deck where the planes landed.

One night, while on the deck, he was standing with another sailor when the cable that caught the planes when landing, snapped. The man standing next to him was significantly injured when the cable hit him. I was amazed by a story that was obviously traumatizing to him but was news to me. So I asked my dad what he did after this. He told me, "After it happened, I walked down to the kitchen and requested a job there."

By asking your parents these types of questions, you'll gain new insights into who they are, and believe me, they'll love talking about it. And for retirees, feel free to open up to

36 http://www.personalhistorians.org

your children and grandchildren about these stories, they'll love hearing about them.

I assure you that you'll not only learn something about them but about yourself as well.

Here's a list of resources that will help people of any age to record their legacy:

- David Solie's Terrific Book, 'How To Say it to Seniors: Closing the Communication Gap with Our Elders"[37]

- Smalltalk Productions – A Documentary Filmmaker Specializing in creating documentaries, oral histories and legacy programming[38]

- Fifty Questions for Family History Interviews[39]

- Association of Personal Historians – find a personal historian to assist you[40]

- The Legacy Project's Life Interview Questions[41]

- 'Seven Questions to Start A Family Legacy Conversation' from Forbes by Ashlea Ebeling[42]

- 'Inheriting Wisdom'[43] products including the fine book, 'The Legacy Conversation'[44]

---

37 http://www.amazon.com/How-Say-It-Seniors-Communication/dp/0735203806

38 http://smalltalkproductions.com

39 http://genealogy.about.com/cs/oralhistory/a/interview.htm

40 http://www.personalhistorians.org/index.php

41 http://www.legacyproject.org/guides/lifeintquestions.pdf

42 http://www.forbes.com/sites/ashleaebeling/2011/01/10/7-questions-to-start-a-family-legacy-conversation/

43 http://www.inheritingwisdom.com/

44 http://www.inheritingwisdom.com/the-legacy-conversation/

- Listing of Questions to create a legacy from Preserving Liberty[45]
- Life Review Questions from Support 4 Change[46]

This section originally appeared on Marketwatch.com - http://www.marketwatch.com/story/the-talk-leaving-a-legacy-in-retirement-2013-02-06

---

45 http://www.preserveliberty.com/LifeInterview.doc

46 http://www.support4change.com/index.php?option=com_content&view=article&id=127&Itemid=169

What About the Empty Nest?

A recent study revealed that the "big happiness boost" for newlyweds lasts only about two years.[47] Those brave souls who last with their partner over two decades can be rewarded with the ability to rediscover their earlier bliss when they reach the freedom of having an empty nest.

The transition from passionate love into something called "companionate love" is a reality and joy for many retirees. My parents were an example of this.

I feared that with all the time that they would be spending together, something could happen. The reality was that something did happen.

To say that my parents were old school would be an understatement. My dad was a New York City sanitation worker and my mom was a nurse. After my sister and I were born, they decided that it was important for one parent to always be at home for us, so they spent the twenty five years following their newlywed two-year period of bliss, working at different times of the day.

---

47 http://www.nytimes.com/2012/12/02/opinion/sunday/new-love-a-short-shelf-life.html?_r=0

My dad worked days picking up garbage on the bowery in New York City and my mom worked nights as a nurse in a busy city hospital's emergency room. Obviously for them it became difficult to rekindle that honeymoon passion on a regular basis.

This reality was the same for so many others, and is the same for so many others still today; after all, life happens. Kids need to be raised. Bills need to be paid. College and retirement funds need to be built up.

Although our family thrived and we always felt loved growing up through all of this, I need to be honest. My parents spent much of their "quality" time bickering; no, actually it was more like arguing. One of their main points of contention was the nightly Yankee game that my dad watched.

Because my dad was very hard of hearing, the volume on the television would regularly disturb my mom's ability to stay asleep before she had to tend to the late night sick at the emergency room. I learned many new and colorful words during those times that my parents "discussed" this issue.

The years went by and both my sister and I found our ways to create our own families and pursue careers. My parents retired and I remember asking friends at my mom's retirement dinner to make sure that they checked in with my mom because I feared that with all the time that they would be spending together, "something" could happen.

The reality was that something did happen. My mom became the biggest Yankee fan you'd ever meet. Her love for Derek Jeter rivaled the love she had for her children and the love she had for her beloved Rags (her dog named after a Yankee pitcher). But it didn't rival the love she had for her husband.

As the retirement years went along, they seemed to be falling back in love. Sure the arguments were there. But they usually ended with a smile and a shrug that indicated that whatever they were arguing about really didn't matter.

A recent article by Sonja Lyubomirsky discusses how many retirees find that their newfound empty nest can often lead to a rediscovery of the "happiness boost" that they had in the early years of their marriage: *"The nest may be empty, but it's also full of possibility for partners to rediscover and surprise each other ... an empty nest offers the possibility of novelty and unpredictability."*[48]

It's amazing that I still am learning life lessons from my parents that can be employed in my later years as well.

This section originally appeared on Marketwatch.com - http://www.marketwatch.com/story/love-retirement-style-2012-12-10

---

48 http://www.nytimes.com/2012/12/02/opinion/sunday/new-love-a-short-shelf-life.html?pagewanted=all&_r=0

How Can You Keep Learning in Retirement?

"Anyone who stops learning is old, whether at 20 or eighty. Anyone who keeps learning stays young. The greatest thing in life is to keep your mind young."

Henry Ford

I recently met a woman at a seminar who told me about the box of books that she had and how she was so excited about her upcoming retirement because she was now going to be able to read all of the books she had saved over the years.

She first started to gather books based on her approach to keeping books that she would want to read on a deserted island and now in retirement, she looked forward to finally reading through her well selected dozen or so books.

A newly retired man told me about his enthusiasm for podcasts about Shakespeare and free online classes from schools like MIT and Stanford. He was particularly excited about starting a class that would require him to read James Joyce's Ulysses, a book that he had fought his entire working life to read. "I'm not sure that I'll understand it," he said, "but at least I'll have the time in retirement to try."

I have written extensively about the need for retirees to take advantage of their time in retirement to continue to learn, both new and old subjects of interest. Retirement can be a time when you can finally study that subject you wanted to in college or really be able to understand Shakespeare or learn what in the heck Einstein was really talking about.

Here are 6 ways in which learning in retirement can bring joy and happiness to retirees:

- Brush the dust off your mind and take a class or read a new genre of literature. Like fiction? Try a nonfiction book that everyone is talking about!

- Take a class. Any kind. It could be at a local college or university. Remember, seniors can take many of these for free or at deeply discounted rates. It could be a cooking class at a restaurant, a poetry class from the library, an herb-growing seminar put on by the local county extension. Even if you're not sure you'll be interested, give it a try. You just never know.

- Turn off the television unless you're watching something that will teach you something you didn't know before. Only watch the minimum of news necessary to know what's going on but don't absorb the negativity.

- Only watching Fox or MSNBC? Try a switch and listen carefully to the opposite side of a debate. Learn why they're saying what they're saying and what positive qualities might exist.

- Talk to new people with an open mind. These can be people who you've never met before and perhaps don't know what your political or other views are. Remember to listen, listen, listen. You may even learn something, including how much you really DO know!

- Make a commitment to learn something new EVERY day.

The need to learn in retirement isn't only for pleasure. Building your brainpower helps your health. Not only extending your life but helping you in the battle against such illnesses as Alzheimer's. Perhaps all of the medical research isn't in yet but there's enough to say that learning rather than sitting will help you to not only enjoy a joyous retirement, but enjoy it for a longer period of time.

Like my two new friends, retirees should try some of these ideas for themselves and they may be surprised at what they'll learn as well.

This section originally appeared on Marketwatch.com - http://www.marketwatch.com/story/6-ways-to-keep-learning-in-retirement-2013-01-17

Do I Need to Visit My Parents Often?

It couldn't happen here!

That's the comment we often hear when a new edict gets handed down from a country such as China. We often scoff at China and similar countries whose government control and draconian measures often reveal their inability to allow freedom and justice to prevail in creating a better society for its people.

So it was for me when I read articles over the last few years about how China was considering laws requiring the adult children of seniors to provide care for their parents. This was based on something that China has always considered to be the "law of the land": filial piety.

Filial piety had been written about by Confucius and many Chinese believe that it is a value that is ingrained in its society. According to Wikipedia, filial piety means *"to be good to one's parents; to take care of one's parents; to perform the duties of one's job well so as to obtain the material means to support parents as well as carry out sacrifices to the ancestors."*[49]

---

49 http://en.wikipedia.org/wiki/Filial_piety

The Wikipedia entry goes on to also point out that filial piety also requires children to "*wisely advise one's parents, including dissuading them from moral unrighteousness.*"[50]

An article in the Wall Street Journal indicates that China is prepared to move forward with a new measure "*urging children to visit their parents and opening the door for elders to sue for better care.*"[51] Yes, the word "sue" is included. I'm not sure what that exactly means in China but I don't think it could be a good thing.

An article in early 2011 reported that the China National Committee on Aging (I wonder what a comparable organization would be in this country) was considering changes to a law that would "*regulate that younger members of society should visit the elderly more often, and the court will have to hear lawsuits about children not visiting parents where previously a court would not accept such actions.*"[52]

So aside from the normal lack of speed getting any regulations created (is China actually that similar to the US?), why is this something that is being instituted now?

The reality in China is that those aged 65 and older now make up over 9% of the population today as compared to 7% as recently as 2010. A recent story that was discussed on social media throughout China focused on the refusal of a local doctor to pay for the medical care of this mother who was in her 70s. Recent research shows that over 50% of China's aging population are "empty nesters" and many in

---

50 ibid

51 http://online.wsj.com/news/articles/SB10001424127887323635504578211118
2817527080

52 http://www.bjreview.com.cn/forum/txt/2011-01/28/content_328988.htm

China believe that their rights can't be effectively protected without legislation.

The quote from Robert England, author of the book, "aging China" from the Wall Street Journal article, is also telling. He states that "*the vast majority of Chinese elderly do not have access to a monthly income provided through a Social Security system. They rely on their children instead to take care of them when they can no longer work. By standing behind this cultural tradition, the government hopes to reduce the number of elderly that may need government-financed care.*"[53]

I'm not sure what to make of this whole matter except to recommend that it's not a bad idea to make a resolution to see your parents more often and when possible provide them worthwhile advice that may include "dissuading them from moral unrighteousness."

The reality is that there are actually laws on the books in this country about filial responsibility,[54] but I don't foresee a need for widespread lawsuits on this matter in our great country. After all, it can't happen here. We take care of our aging population here, don't we?

This section originally appeared on Marketwatch.com - http://www.marketwatch.com/story/visit-your-parents-or-risk-being-sued-2013-01-08

---

53 http://online.wsj.com/news/articles/SB100014241278873236355045782111 82817527080

54 http://graphics8.nytimes.com/packages/pdf/health/NOA/30states.pdf

What is The Secret to a Longer Retirement?

As you know at this point, I believe that there are "Four Keys" to living a long and safe retirement.

Obviously all retirements depend upon having a solid financial foundation and fortunately there are many resources (including writers on this site and working with qualified financial advisors) available to help you to achieve this (although there is no substitute for saving and investing wisely).

It's also vital that you consider two other "keys" as well—health and mental attitude—in any planning for, and discussions about, retirement and your later life.

Before I get into the fourth key—and it's a critical one to consider for all in or planning on retirement—let me take you to an actual island called Ikaria.

The following is an excerpt from my book, ***"Having The Talk" The Four Keys to Your Parents' Safe Retirement"***[55] *about the tight-knit community on Ikaria that has such a history of longevity that researchers have gathered to unravel their secret:*

---

55 http://talk.peopletested.com

"So far, studies show the people on Ikaria[56] reach the ripe old age of 90 at two-and-a-half times the rate of Americans, with men at four times the rate of their American counterparts. As well, the onset of chronic illness such as heart disease and cancer is delayed in Ikaria by up to ten years, and dementia sets in at only 25% the rate it does here in the States. Not only do these island inhabitants live longer, but they live healthier, too.

"Could it just be all that healthy Mediterranean food and fresh Aegean air? Apparently, it's not. On a neighboring island, just over nine miles away, the longevity rate is much lower than on Ikaria, and the onset of chronic illness arrives earlier, much like in America. Something else is at work.

"The diet on Ikaria supports longer and healthier living, and is heavy in fresh vegetables, including wild greens, as well as potatoes and beans, while low in dairy and red meat. However, these factors alone aren't enough to explain the much higher longevity combined with better health on this remote island. The answer appears to be in another category altogether, and this has proven to be true in other pockets of high longevity.

"The people on Ikaria have a deeply knit social structure; everyone contributes to his or her community in some way. You're expected to. It's simply the way they live, even if it's just a matter of growing a garden and sharing the proceeds. Almost every evening, people gather and drink wine, relate stories, and relax friends. It's this deep connection with other people that researchers are beginning to believe is the secret ingredient for longevity when combined with a healthy

56 http://www.nytimes.com/2012/10/28/magazine/the-island-where-people-for-get-to-die.html?pagewanted=all&_r=2&

lifestyle. And it's this deep social connection that is the fourth key to your parent's safe retirement.

The Japanese use the word ikigai to describe "the reason for which you get out of bed." This is the same idea. When you have a healthy social structure, you have a sense of purpose and belonging.

"Dan Buettner, who reported on Ikaria for the New York Times, wrote that 'as soon as you take culture, belonging, purpose or religion out of the picture, the foundation for long healthy lives collapses. The power of such an environment lies in the mutually reinforcing relationships among lots of small nudges and default choices.[57] "

As I also learned from my own research and personal experiences and which I documented in my first book, "**Safe 4 Retirement: The Four Keys to a Safe Retirement,**"[58] the necessity to stay involved by creating and nurturing your own social network is that fourth Key to creating a longer and safer retirement.

This section originally appeared on Marketwatch.com - http://www.marketwatch.com/story/the-talk-secret-to-a-longer-retirement-2013-02-14

---

57 http://www.nytimes.com/2012/10/28/magazine/the-island-where-people-forget-to-die.html?pagewanted=all&_r=2&
58 http://safe.peopletested.com

How Important is Social Networking for Retirees?

The fourth key aspect of the talk and having a safe and long retirement is the need to stay involved. The building and nurturing of a strong social network for retirees is vital to their own longevity and their ability to weather the storms that will occur with later life.

For the adult child of a retired or retiring parent, part of the emphasis during the talk should be on making sure your parents don't succumb to loneliness or isolation during their retirement and later years. They need to develop and nurture a satisfying social network. For your parents to truly thrive in their golden years, which means not only having more fun but also living longer and healthier lives, they need to build and maintain a web of friends and family. You can play a vital role in this process.

Your parents may be naturally social, and when you explain the health and longevity advantages, they may become even more so. For others, your parents lean toward the hermit side, or perhaps, upon retiring, they seem to have lost their sense of worth and perceived place in society. Here you can step in with not only educating them on the importance of a social network, but also setting the example.

The reality is that in retirement, people will lose friends and loved ones. Unfortunately, a common occurrence in retirement and later life is the loss of a spouse. Family members must be on alert for what is known as the "broken heart" syndrome,[59] which occurs after the death of one spouse and the partner soon passes away as well. However, many avoid this syndrome and become resilient after the loss of a spouse by utilizing their social network for strength, compassion and support.

One of the most important things that adult children can do with their parents during the talk is to stress the importance of creating and strengthening their social network with friends (those that they know and those that they haven't met yet), loved ones, church members, etc.

But don't forget what you can do as a part of the family. Invite them to family events and engage them fully in family activities—dinners, movies, outings with the grandkids. The family relationship is often the most critical element of their social network.

Here are some questions that you can ask your retiring parents during the talk to ensure that you cover the all important fourth key, the need to stay involved:

1) Will you stay involved with colleagues from work?

2) What key recreational activities (like golf, tennis, bridge, and opera) do you plan on doing?

---

59 http://safe4retirement.com/is-it-common-for-a-spouse-to-die-so-soon-after-the-loss-of-the-other-spouse/

3) How involved will you be with your kids and grand-kids?

4) What circle of friends do you want to nurture and spend more time with?

5) Will you volunteer in your community or with a national or international organization?

6) What new hobbies will you take up?

7) If you're single, will you look for another life partner?

8) Will you continue to work in your retirement even if you don't need to financially?

9) Will you take classes and continue to grow intellectually?

The need to stay involved is not only about protecting your parents from the realities of what will occur in retirement and later life. Rather, the need to stay involved and having a strong social network will provide them the ability to share the joys and fun of their retirement with others.

Just like your parents were most content when they knew that you, their child, was happy, so it'll be for you when you look at your parents living a full and long retirement and realizing that they're happy and fulfilled.

Believe me, it'll bring a smile to your face.

This section originally appeared on Marketwatch.com - http://www.marketwatch.com/story/the-talk-social-networking-vital-for-retirees-2013-02-19

Should My Parents Move Closer to Me?

The value of having and maintaining a strong social structure is critical to the happiness and longevity of those in retirement.

A strong social structure is built upon the foundation of friends and family members who help to support, nurture, entertain and bring joy into the lives of those enjoying their "golden years."

Many of us considering retirement spend time reading the columns that discuss the "best places to retire" We're told to look for towns or even countries, where there's warm weather, lots of activities and opportunities for retirees to continue to grow and learn, such as living in college towns. These decisions must also include consideration of existing social connections and the opportunity for continuing to grow one's social network as well.

As Jack Hansen and Jerry Haas point out in their well researched and readable book, "**Shaping a Life of Significance for Retirement**"[60], the move to a dream location

---

60 http://www.amazon.com/Shaping-Life-Significance-Retirement-Hansen/
dp/0835810259/ref=sr_1_1?s=books&ie=UTF8&qid=1365446065&sr=1-1&key-
words=shaping+a+life+of+significance+for+retirement

in retirement can turn into a nightmare. They state, "*The nightmare quality often hinges on their having left behind a network of friends with appreciating the difficulty of building a new one or a clear idea of how to go about it. In retirement, as in other phases of adult life, significant friendships are critical to a sense of connectedness and fulfillment.*"

In their book, Hansen and Haas spent much time talking to retirees and their book has findings based upon their research that shows real life experiences that provide lessons for everyone either in, or planning for retirement. The authors report that half of the people they spoke to had relocated in retirement.

Most had moved "back" to communities where they had lived and reconnected with friends and a community that they knew. Of these, there were many stories of retirees returning to communities where many of their old friends were no longer living and many found that they had to build "new" friendships as if they had relocated to an area that was "new" to them.

This was a similar experience for those who had moved to new communities who Hansen and Haas found the concern that it's "*harder to break into a well established community because people's 'relationship plate' is already pretty full.*"

When considering relocation in retirement or in one's later years, what we often see is the well meaning adult children encouraging their parents to relocate closer to a community that they knew and built: their own family.

Many retirees relish the ability to enjoy time in retirement with their grandchildren. This can create much joy not only for the retiree and the grandchild, but it can also satisfy a need for the adult children who has a loved one who can assist with the parenting needs of young children. Many view the return of retirees to either the home or neighborhood of their adult children as a "win win" for everyone.

But is it really?

This is obviously one of those items that is a personal decision and there can be no blanket statements about it being right or wrong for everyone. Everyone's situation is different and that is how it should be evaluated.

It's important for both the adult children and the parents to understand the importance of the social structure that's needed to support retirees as they age. There are wonderful benefits for being around their children and grandchildren but if this move puts them into a new neighborhood where they've left the friends and social connections that have been nurturing them, it may not be the right move. It could cripple the social structure that they've built and ultimately have an adverse impact of them.

When considering the move "back home with family," the following questions should be considered by the adult child before it's recommended to a parent:

1. Do I need to have my parent closer to home because of their health concerns?

2. Is this more about making something convenient for me or is it what's best for my parent?

3. Is there a risk that this arrangement could damage the relationship with my parents and counteract any of the rewards that could be gained from it?

4. Will there be a social structure beyond just our family that my parents can tap into and nurture that will benefit them?

As Hansen and Haas found in their book, *"for the majority of individuals (who had relocated), a feeling of 'being at home' in a community seemed to have more to do with significant friendships than with proximity to family members."*

This section originally appeared on Marketwatch.com - http://www.marketwatch.com/story/locating-near-family-not-always-the-best-move-2013-04-09

Special Offer

In appreciation for your purchase of this book, I'd like to provide you a special offer on a home study course that will help you and your parents to achieve a safe retirement.

I'm providing a **50% off special** on this course, **Your Safe Retirement Package**.

This package includes the following:

- Full copies of my books, "**Safe 4 Retirement: The Four Keys to a Safe Retirement**" and "**The 10 Joys of a Safe Retirement**"
- Many hours of audio and video lessons on how to achieve a safe retirement
- Extensive excerpts from books including my book, "**Having The Talk: The Four Keys to Your Parents' Safe Retirement**" and Gordon Filepas' "**Lean and Healthy to 100**"
- Full versions of classic books including "**Think and Grow Rich**", "**As A Man Thinketh**", "**Siddhartha**" and many others
- Thousands of recipes
- A full one hour webinar on "**Breaking the Silence & Information Barrier Within Families**"

AND MUCH MORE

- Plus, you will receive **a full PDF version of this book** that you can use for your own purposes, or to forward to family or friends.

To take advantage of this offer, please go to the special URL:

http://YourSafeRetirementPackage.com

About the Author

Jack Tatar

Jack Tatar is known as "America's Safe Retirement Coach" and is the author of books that are changing how people view retirement.

His first, "Safe *4 Retirement: The Four Keys to a Safe Retirement*[61]" lays out his foundational approach to viewing retirement in a holistic fashion by including the Four Keys: Financial Preparedness, Health & Wellness, Mental Attitude and Staying Involved into planning for retirement.

His latest book is "Having *The Talk: The Four Keys to Your Parents' Safe Retirement*[62]", which lays out the need and plan for having that necessary "talk" between retired or retiring parents, and their children and family about later life issues.

He writes regularly for Marketwatch.com as one of their RetireMentors.

Jack's contact information:
Website: www.safe4retirement.com
Email: Jack@safe4retirement.com
LinkedIn: www.linkedin.com/in/jacktatar/
Twitter: http://twitter.com/Safe4Retirement
Facebook: http://facebook.com/Safe4Retirement

---

61 http://safe.peopletested.com

62 http://talk.peopetested.com

For more information on Jack's resources to achieve a safe retirement, please go to

http://RetireSafelyLiveLonger.com

If you have any stories of your own on this topic, I'd love to hear them.

Please email them to me at Jack@Safe4Retirement.com

For more information on other books in the "What's the Deal...?" **series**

Please visit People Tested Publications at

http://www.PeopleTested.com

or write us at

Info@PeopleTested.com

www.ingramcontent.com/pod-product-compliance
Lightning Source LLC
Chambersburg PA
CBHW070555030426
42337CB00016B/2511